In the Fragrance of Frangipanis

A Collection of Poetry

Puja Roy

I am a touch and breath away,
In the fragrance of frangipanis,
The salt of the ocean,
The flow of the brook.

Contents

Contents

Foreword

Writing this foreword is harder than I expected it to be. Being able to shed some light on the person my mother was in only a couple of paragraphs seems a near-Sisyphean task because there will always be more I could say about her. But it is important that people reading this book know about her and who she was, so I will do my best, and trust that the poems in these pages will do their part to fill in the gaps.

My mother, Puja Roy, was the most compassionate and empathetic person I've ever known. She was always the first to go out of her way to be there for someone who needed it, be it family, friend, or stranger. Along with this inherently selfless drive to help others, or perhaps forged directly by it, came a rock-solid sense of justice and the courage to pursue it. Right from her mid-twenties in the 1980s, my mother dove into the murky waters of fighting for women's rights in India. This was not a field that one entered for recognition or wealth, but for more than 35 years, my mother braved the opposing storm of tradition and misogyny that plagues women and girls in this country. She started as a counselor, and then as a consultant, working with various organisations and NGOs, each of which was focused on the struggle for the rights of women and girls. Over the years, she spent weeks and months in various places all over South Asia, from remote villages in India to the towns and cities of Nepal, Bhutan, and Sri Lanka. Her work covered everything from actively combating the trafficking of women to fundraising for girls' football teams in small Indian villages to shedding light on the archaic practice of witch hunting that still exists today. Most recently, she spent several years working with an organisation to eradicate child marriage in Jharkhand and improve access to education for the girls there.

All this is just a fraction of what she was able to accomplish, and doesn't yet touch on her personal life. At home, she was our rock. She was never reserved with words of affection, and when she laughed, her smile lit up the room. We always knew what love was because of her, and my sister, father, and I are better people for having known her. From her, I received a love for books and for writing. At home, it was rare to find her without a book in her hand.

I think it was perhaps this rare combination of an affinity for words and an unwavering moral compass that led to most of the poems in this book. Some of the poems are more intimate, and about herself or her loved ones. Others deal with injustices she noticed around her, and her thoughts on the lives of women in society. And others still are more carefree observations, or hopeful calls for the future. A large number of these poems were first written by hand as far back as the early 1990s. The rest were written over the years that followed, and some of the more recent ones were even posted online. None of these poems have been edited for content, and have been directly transcribed from the medium they were originally written in, physical or digital. Either way, I hope you are able to enjoy these poems for what they are and that they lend some more insight into the strong, radiant woman that was my mother.

With love,
Anubhav Roy Bhattacharya

To You

Love

Two ordinary people,
Special and beautiful,
To each other…
Two people,
Sharing, a life unique,
A time immortal.
Two people,
Discovering themselves,
As one…
Two people, ordinary
But intense,
Common, yet rare,
Creating a secluded
Cocoon of understanding,
Believing in themselves,
And each other,
Stretching time,
In an embrace…
Called love.

The Feather Touch

Have you ever felt
The touch
Of a
Feather?
Have you ever felt
A caress
So light
A thought
So gentle
A revelation
So bright
That its
Essence permeates
Every nerve
Every breath
Of your
Understanding?
A wonder
Which touches you
For a
Moment of…
Eternity.

Our Rhythm

I appreciate your humour,
He said.
I like the way you converse,
Your head tilted to the side,
Your words, witty, terse.
I understand your brooding silences,
He mused.
The frown upon your face,
When you struggle with your conscience,
And gauge society's pace.
When we are together,
I know,
The world that we have
Is our own.
But when we travel
Through closed fists and doors,
We know our freedom's flown.
But we have each other,
You say,
Surely that's enough?
But to slow ourselves
To the establishment's tread…
It promises to be rough.

I Will Shine a Light

"This is dedicated to all of you who have daughters! Shine a light on their dreams!"

– Puja Roy

The moment I saw you
The moment you smiled
The moment
You leapt into my arms
And into my life
I wondered
How I could feel
Such abundance, an overflow
Of love, warmth, tenderness?

I have a daughter?
Yes, I have a daughter!
I'm awestruck…
I have a daughter!
An incredible adventure
Of love and laughter,
So much promise
A world of wonder!

You, my dear girl,
How I wanted you,
How can I ever explain

The desire
To hold you…
The desire to
Hold your hand
All the way,
Leading you safely
Through the arduous
Paths of life…

And I shook myself
I reminded myself
Firmly
You have your
Own dreams
They are not mine to mould,
Your dreams are for you
Yours to nurture,
Yours to behold.
And I will never
Tread on your dreams
But I will shine a light…

I will shine a light for you
Onto those arduous paths…
I will shine a light
And help you see
Who you are
And who you will be.

My promise to you
My resilient, wondrous spirit,
Is not to shove you
Onto one path
But to shine a light
For you to see
The path of your dreams,
Not to enclose you
Within the walls of limitation
But to throw open
Your doors of freedom and imagination.

So grasp your dreams,
Free your thoughts,
And one day, my dear child,
You will be a guiding light…
For someone else
To find her way.

For My Precious Daughter

You bounced into my life
A shiny, bubbly, effervescent star
I had searched for you
And there you were
Resplendent in oversized yellow;
    (A yellow dress, yellow bow, yellow socks!)
You wore (along with all that yellow!)
A beaming smile
That enquired
"Where have you been all my life, mummy?"
I made a promise that day,
That proud day when I found myself a daughter,
To not smother you,
To not hold you back,
To not say,
"You can't do this!"
And heaven forbid…
To not say,
"You can't do this because you are a girl!"
I made a promise that day
To help you
Unfold
Grow
Blossom…
Into A Person

With strong views
Into a Woman
With her own voice
Into an Individual
Who would question and challenge
Despite fears of rejection
Who would find her voice
Who would not be subdued
By our peculiar environment called culture.
And I see in you
As you grow
Shimmers of a leader
Glimmers of a promise
To be
As you are...
That special, unique star.

Love you,
Mummy

Not a Princess

"Treating a daughter like a 'princess' in our culture does not necessarily mean freedom for the so-called princess. And in real life, princesses are bound by strict rules of conduct. This is in response to the princess craze among young girls; no real harm, but they can be so much more than just an idea of a glamorous princess. This poem is for my daughter who is happiest on the soccer field and who will never have her world restricted by binding social norms."

– Puja Roy, July 22, 2016

You are a streak of sunshine,
On a grey and misty day.
Racing through the sodden field,
You know you'll find a way.
You are happiest on this field,
Sprinkled with pools and puddles.
You are sunniest (despite dreary drizzles!),
Breaking free of all your hurdles.

I watch you with abundant pride,
I see a person, not a princess with rules to abide.
You are a young, carefree spirit,
Marching, meandering through life,
At your own pace in your own stride.
You are not a princess,
With a set path to follow.

You own your voice, have a choice,
Live a life you don't have to borrow.

You live in a world,
Where there'll always be,
A closing door, a rising wall.
"Protecting" girls from a dishonourable fall.
Don't be a princess who is scared to fall,
Reach out, stretch out,
Open the door…and scale the wall.

You are a streak of sunshine,
In this drizzling, dreary field,
Find a shining life to build,
And to that closed, cloistered princess' life?
I know you will not yield!

———•◆•———

I Will Hold You

"This is in memory of my father who left us more than 17 years ago. It took me years to come to terms with the way he left and I'd start writing something and then leave it unfinished because it was too painful and I wasn't ready. Now, more than 17 years later, I have put something down which I am sure everyone will relate to in different ways. Today is not his death anniversary, nor is it his birth anniversary; it is just a day that I remembered him strongly and decided to write about him. This poem of remembrance is dedicated to all of you who have lost special, loved ones in your lives.......no experience of loss is the same; by sharing mine I'm hoping that somewhere there are common thoughts and emotions to hold on to."

– Puja Roy, November 12, 2017

It was too early
Your mind so strong
You went so suddenly
It feels so wrong.
I watched you suffer
As you struggled to breathe
How I longed to reach
Into your ebbing soul…
How I yearned to share your pain
Willing you
To control your life again…

Your hand, your mind…always there for me
No matter how strong our disagreements could be…
Just this once, I pleaded, hold on to ME…
My voice, my thoughts, echoed mindlessly
Against the dark, emptying sanctum of your mind
As you faded away silently…
This is not happening……..not this way
There's still so much I have to say.

And those days you lay there
Far away from this existence,
I wished I could open the doors
One last time,
To reach closer, to share, to KNOW.
Did you hear my voice, feel my touch
Did you see a light
That willed you to fight?

We had understood each other
Through small touches
Some words, silences, and a bond
Made not always out of agreement
But of consideration, and….love .
And as you lay still…
I don't know why you went
I don't know where you are…
And through the meaningless mire
Of confusion, of zero reason, of futility…

I will hold you and all you meant

I will keep you and continue to be

I will treasure you and strive to see…

Where this mysterious life of mine leads me.

I will hold you always…..I will hold you.

Special

"I know that this is not friendship day, but friendship doesn't have to have a special day. This is for all my friends; I hope you can relate to it and share it with those whose friendship you value beyond words."

– Puja Roy, August 16, 2014

Sitting in silence,
Sharing every thought,
An eternal understanding,
Always there, never sought.

Years and miles apart,
Remote destinies and lives,
And still our warmth and light,
Shimmers and survives.

I walk to your door,
Several light years later,
I wonder, will you think,
"Oh how she's changed, and not for the better?"

The door opens and we embrace,
Not in a sliver of light,
But a beacon of splendour
That time and distance
Couldn't erase or devour.

We know...we will always know,
That we share
An infinite bond
Of brilliance, warmth and care...

Special understanding, special thought...
    Always there...
        And never sought.

To Me

Reflections on Ambition

Do I want to be successful?
Yes.
For whom?
For me, of course.
Really?
Well…maybe for others too.
For whom?
For all those I love.
Only them?
For all those who are helped by
Whatever I did to become successful.
So I want to be famous?
Not exactly.
No?
Well…maybe well known.
Why?
I want to DO something BIG for
SOMEONE and get KNOWN in the
Process.
Ultimately for whom?
For me…of course.

Tongue-tied, Mind-tied

I want to say
What I mean
For it is important
To me
To say
What I mean.
And when I say it
My words tumble over
Each other
Because I'm so scared
They won't listen.
So before they stop listening,
I try to get my words out
So they get to listen,
But because I get my
Words tumbling out,
They don't listen
Anyway…..
So….
I'm always so scared
To say what I mean
Because
They
Don't
Listen.

————•●•————

The Gap

Why don't I get across what I mean?
To know that what I say is true
To my understanding.
I know that my thoughts
Are mine to express freely…
And so often, so often,
They are ground to the dust
By people who
Don't care to understand
I think that people differ
So much
In perceptions,
That every perception
Should be respected.

Moment of Truth

I sometimes, no, very often,
Wish that I had the energy
To fight for what I feel
Is right,
But at the last moment,
My confidence fails me;
People always seem to get
The better of me;
I know it's not because
I don't feel strongly;
I do; but my mind
Is a mass of confusion,
Seething with unsorted
Thoughts.
I don't do what I know
I can do; I let myself get
Walked over, and then replay the
Incident in my mind; favouring
Myself.
Maybe I don't care enough about
myself.
Protect myself.
From some unknown, perhaps fictitious
force.

For this is where I question…
Will I keep doing this
To myself?
Perhaps I will.

No One

All alone
All alone,
Every point
Drives it home,
Whatever I say
Whatever I think,
Only I know
What I mean.
However much
I show of
myself,
A thought misunderstood,
Cannot be replaced.
For people think
What they want
To think,
They don't care
Anything
For what I think,
And I retreat
All alone
To the understanding
Which I understand…
Alone.

Drowned Self

I reached out
With a trembling hand
And clutched the confusion
And rage which had
Burst forth
Like a broken dam
Threatening destruction
To no one
But myself.
Words that jab, tear, tease,
Mercilessly.
Looks that taunt, jeer and say,
"You can't do anything about it."
Attitudes that leave a hole of
Aching pain, of nagging doubt,
A skeleton of self,
A self without conviction
A self which hides
A self which runs
From its own shadow.
A self which forgets
That there is a world outside,
And in doing so,
Drowns its identity.

Individuality

I stand alone
In a sea of masked strangers.
I feel my strength
At the fall of an axe
Or at the troubled voice of my
Conscience,
When I think
Of all those times when
Choices were left to me
There had to be a reason,
A valid reason
For acting the way I did
And for turning my back
On scornful voices and faces
In a world where only I
Know that no one else
Matters but myself.

——•——

Moving Thoughts

I feel what I write.
I see the words
Slowly disentangle
From a mass
Of confusion
And spring forth
With surprising
Alacrity and agility
Into the gallery
Of my thoughts
And in that fleeting
Time, I see a world
That is mine
Alone,
To feel
The way I want to,
Freedom to see
What I feel for,
The beauty of the
Self
Coming alive.

My Power

January 26, 2022

I discover
within me,
Hidden wells of power
Sparkling moments of discovery,
Intense, exciting yet serene.
And in these glorious moments
of self-realisation,
I diminish no-one;
My power is my own,
Ensconced within,
My freedom is mine,
To realise and affirm.

My Freedom

"Written for the #whyloiter movement on claiming public spaces."

– Puja Roy, December 17, 2014

Curious eyes,
Follow my footsteps
As I meander barefoot
In the park,
Through luscious, forbidden grass,
As it slowly grows dark...
I sit alone,
In a sea
Of hostile strangers
Who glare and snicker
At my solitary self
And my solitary dinner.
And I stare at them all,
My eyes say:
I will stand tall
I am free
I am in charge
Can't you see?
I am energised, thrilled,
Peaceful and strong,
Know that the pleasure I seek

Can never be wrong
I will wander,
I will meander,
I will feel pleasure
And I will loiter
For my freedom is not yours to give
But mine to take,
Mine to feel
And mine to make.

Puja

I am a descendant of magnificent, nurturing,
    and caring women of Bengal.

My mother, an independent thinker, a soul of strength,
    a poet, and songwriter, raised me and
Her quiet strength and free spirit inspired, nourished,
    and grew me.

I am the smell of hope in abundance,
    a warrior who has fought many battles.

I am the sound of sea waves, of an infinity
    that stretches into the horizon.

My name is Puja.

A Woman's Mind: A Collection of Thoughts

Puja Roy

A Tentative Thought

Isn't it strange
How often
One apologises
For being hurt?
The person who hurts
Thinks I shouldn't be hurt,
So I feel sorry
For being hurt
And I apologise to the
Person
For hurting me

To the MCP

You think you own
The world
With all its women.
Look around you
She smiles up
At your feet.
Sit in your makeshift
Throne and survey
The illusion around you.
Yes sir, you feel you
Have it all.
You have the women
But they can't have you.
You have a wife
She does what you say,
You have a mistress,
She does what you say,
You have a mother
She knows she has to do
What you say
You have a daughter
Of course she does what
You say
They don't say anything
For you to do

For they feel they don't
Have anything to offer you
And you feel they can't
Offer you anything
For they don't own you
And they won't ever
Own you
And you feel you own
Yourself…
But take a hammer
And shatter that
Thick glass
With some well chosen
Blows of hard thought,
For the man who
Can't share is
A thing of pity
And pity is the lowest form of
Humiliation,
And you can't share
Your thoughts
Your love
Your ideas
With another woman
So you are a thing
Of pity.
You think of a woman
Far removed

From your line of thought
A necessary part of life
Perhaps
But not quite in your
Superior class.
You don't want to understand
How a woman thinks
How she feels
You don't want to see
What she sees
You want to go ahead
With life
Feeling you are life
But you are missing out
On half your life.
You can't share,
You can't understand,
You can't see
You have only half a life
You can't be
The human being
Man should be.
You are an MCP.

To the Woman In Me

I have this burning drive
      Called ambition.
A sinking fear
      Of humiliation,
The ambition of identification,
      Of destination,
A gnawing dread
      Of failures past…
And future.

Positive Strength

Woman?
What do you think of?
Battered, subdued,
Secondary, dowry,
Burnt, silenced,
Widowed, wife,
Daughter, submissive,
Sex, reproduction,
Domestic, housewife…
And the list is
Endless.
And when we keep asking…
Woman? Woman? Woman?
We keep searching,
Searching,
And there it is…
A person, an individual,
Feelings, love, strength,
Compassion, endless,
Composed…
A well of determination
Stretching on to…
Eternity.

More Like a Man?

Remember what Rex Harrison
Sang
In "My Fair Lady?"
"Why can't a woman
Be more like a man?"
But the <u>real</u> question is:
"Why can't a woman
Be more like
Herself?"
Strong, indomitable, free.
Instead, she's a shadow
Of Herself,
Living in a world
Created by a man
Who thinks
She can't fight back
Because <u>she</u> <u>feels</u>
She can't fight back
Because she feels
That what she's fighting for
Is not hers to fight for,
Because what she wants
And doesn't fight for,
    Is…
        Herself.

Warped Pride

She was raped
But she never spoke
For it would hurt
Her pride.
She was molested,
But she never let on
For it would damage
Her pride.
She was harassed
But told
Not to protest
For it would shatter
Her pride.
A husband was
To be bought
For her,
But she was told
To swallow her pride
To protect the pride
That would
Make her a bride.
And she protected & protected
& protected her pride

Until she saw
That the pride
Which she thought was pride
Was no longer pride.

Reflections on
Pavement Life

Strong and Withered

She was bent double
Wrapped in rags
Firmly clinging
To two parts
Of her
Spent life..
Symbols of
What was left…
And what was to be…
A stained begging bowl
A twisted walking stick
Clinging on to them
Purposefully,
Determinedly,
Confident…
For some reason…
To survive.

Alone

I wonder where
She came from
I wonder where
She belongs.
Did she have a past?
A life of laughter?
A life of sorrow?
Of ambition?
Of confusion?
All that is gone
But not forgotten,
As she sits
On a filthy sheet,
A burnt pot
With remnants
Of yesterday's meal.
Smouldering…
On a half doused fire,
Ashes scattered nearby,
A woman, still young,
With the remnants of a life,
A story which no one cares to know,
A tale she has lived through…
Alone.

Puja Roy

Futile Dreams

A broken doll
A torn flower
Half a biscuit
A tattered cover
Laughing voices
Playful minds
Running feet
Where are the binds?
Into a halting train
They climb
Little hands, little voices, little feet
Two worlds meet
The ragged children in ragged clothes
See the women frown in well made robes
The women alight
The train's empty
He looks around
Weariness creeps
Silently stretches
And in a minute,
Fast asleep.

Despair and Hope

He caught every
Passerby,
Saying, "Aunty I'm hungry",
And aunty passed him by,
Thinking, "He's an
Addict, or part
Of a gang, or
He'll pick my pocket,
Snatch my purse,
Or he'll give the
Money to the leader,
So what's the use?"
So she hurries on by.
He stares after her,
Lost, confused, lonely,
Hurt and despair in his
Eyes. Until…
The next aunty comes by,
And with
Hope in his eyes,
He hurries after her,
Saying, "Aunty, I'm hungry."

⸺ ·●· ⸺

Puja Roy

Breakfast Time

"Observations from my house to the swimming pool."

– Puja Roy, Calcutta, July 1991

A fresh day
A bright spirit
A hearty step
I think I felt it,
The life in every source,
And I saw her,
Bread bag in mouth,
Romping steadily on.
Destination?
The little ones
Under the steel frame
Of a car,
Who, squealing excitedly,
Gathered around her,
And she dropped the packet,
Watched proudly from a distance,
Her little family of puppies
Feasting…
For it was…
Breakfast time.

The World Around Me

The Family Meal

They sat together,
Huddled.
A baby wailed,
Not cuddled.
He marched in
Peremptorily,
Demanded & knew
It was his.
A privilege that is a man's,
A right to be served first
With the best…
She stood by
Respectfully, fearfully.
The wails carried on.
An impatient gesture,
The wails stopped.
They knew the boss.
He finished, stretched,
Walked out slowly.
Not another word.
Sighs of relief….
Now the family
Could sit down
To a well-earned meal.

The Return

"This is a poetic account of an incident I experienced when I was a child. I witnessed how a relative was sent back to an abusive marriage because no one felt she had any choice but to return. They all knew she wasn't independent, that she was abused, but she never received any real support from anyone. I remember that I, as a child, felt helpless and extremely aware of a sense of injustice although I wasn't exactly able to comprehend the full situation.

Today, unfortunately, in our culture, marriage is still sacrosanct, an institution which is prioritized over an individual's happiness and freedom. So many women still face physical, psychological abuse in marital relationships and don't receive support from their families to extricate themselves. And there are dire consequences to remaining in violent circumstances like an abusive relationship.

I hope that my childhood reminiscences will strike a chord of awareness among those who know of women living with violence and are silent about it. Let's spread the message and break the silence."

– Puja Roy, September 9, 2018

He came for her
The monster clad in white
An alarming, fearsome sight.
He pounded in and bellowed
"Get ready, we'll leave soon,

We have to go while it's afternoon."
The women rushed to prepare her leave,
It was the end of her reprieve.

Darkness filled the eyes, once full of light.
They sent a silent, desperate plea
To the women and men who would not see
Her painful, sorrowful plight…
There was nothing I could do
To make things right.

Her feet leaden, eyes swollen
She was told, "Go where you belong!"
With all my heart, I, a child, knew that to be wrong.

Little whispers of protest
Buzzed away with impatience
"No, she cannot stay,
What will people say?
She's married now,
She'll manage somehow."

Her eyes held no hope
Silent and resigned
All her dreams and desires
Which marriage had denied.

"Feed him well, then leave,
You are his wife

This is your life,
That's what you have to believe."

The monster preened with command,
Her hands fulfilled his every demand.
Clad in white and an indelible smirk,
(He knew what he was worth!)
His voluminous clothes stretched
Over a conspicuous girth.

Cross-legged, he demolished
Rich, decadent offerings
With swollen, ring-adorned fingers.
And with each devoured mouthful
She watched hope and her life disappear…
The monster ate it all; it was so very painful.

There was nothing I could do
To change the wrong and make things right.

The monster stretched, slow and satisfied,
Smirk in place; a deprecating, challenging glare,
At all those who dared to stare…

She collected herself, her body, mind and bag.
Freedom, she knew, was an unaffordable tag.
Her head held high, dry-eyed and silent,
She followed his impatient beckoning,
I wondered, why is she not defiant?

Purposeful, leaden steps…as she disappears,
Oblivious to their whispers and tears.
Empty. Futile. Meaningless.
"You are his wife.
You have no life,"
The words echoed in their hollow embraces.

They left in their wake, smudges of
Sorrow, shame, bitterness,
Helplessness, guilt, and emptiness.
A heavy shadow over a day sunny and bright,
And there was nothing, nothing at all I could do
To make it right.

The Forbidden Swing

"This story, in verse, is based on an incident in our building where children, whose parents work in the building, were not allowed to use the park. They stay in a slum rehabilitation building next door where there is no access to playgrounds. This is very similar to the situation where maids and workers have to use only the service lift in our building. I decided to write about it as a way of raising some awareness on this and some understanding so that hopefully there will soon be a bridge between the 'special' people and those not considered special at all."

– Puja Roy, June 14, 2017

He watched the squealing children
On swings that flew high
His eyes followed
The special ones
As they chased Each Other
With Easy Abandon
Over ladders and
Whoosh! Down a slide
That curved and curved
Until the bump of sand
And he could almost feel the breeze,
Sift the sand between little fingers…
He watched until
The slides were free and the

Swings rocked in empty silence…
With longing and hopelessness.

"I'm going next door," she said,
"Come with me." And he followed
Her into the building for special people…
And they rode the lift,
Not the special one for special people,
But the large one with its cardboard floor
For servants and garbage,
Dogs and baggage.
The door opened and Madam said,
"Sit in the kitchen, let your sister work."

He looked out the window,
Saw the empty swings
Staring.
He got up, with sudden decision,
Sailing down in breathless excitement
(In the garbage lift, of course!)
He was in the park,
A lonely figure,
Furtive and silent…
But the breeze was on his face,
Swinging high on the forbidden swing,
Whoosh! The thrilling, winding slide,
Bump! Onto the sand and the grains were real
Running through his fingers. He got up

For another go…
The voice was scary, impossibly loud…
"What are you doing?
Go away!
You know you cannot play!"
Rough hands grabbed and pulled,
"Let me go," he gasped, "My sister is here."
"Don't you know," the loud voice spat,
"This park is not for you, you brat?"
"There are rules, you must obey,
So just go away!"
The man watched grimly…
The forlorn figure disappeared.

"Don't you know, you silly child,"
She shouted, "There are places
We cannot go, things we cannot do?"
"Why?" asked the bewildered voice,
"I only wanted to play,
When everyone was away!"
Her voice was soft and sad,
"There are different worlds for them and us,
Stay in our world, don't grow your dreams,
For one day, they will be too big, and you will
Still be small."

He stared out the window,
And he was riding the swing,

Higher and higher,
Faster and faster,
Until the blur, the crash…
And he didn't feel anymore.

Don't

"I just thought I would share this with you. It's a poem I wrote about my ongoing fight with my building management for discriminating against maids and household helpers."

– Puja Roy

Don't use our lift
There's a separate one for you
Don't use our loo
There's one outside for you
Don't use our plates
Here's yours and a cup too
Don't sit in our chairs
(But do clean and dust them well)
Don't take a sick day
You won't get your pay
Don't raise your voice
Remember, you don't have a choice
We will give you clothes
We will give you food
Some medicines perhaps,
Bonus money too,
But don't ask
For dignity
Don't ask for privilege

You are,
A different class
There are certain things
We can't give
And you can't take
We have taught our children this
For heaven's sake!
What did you say?
Discrimination? Apartheid?
Don't be ridiculous!
We are practical, realistic,
We are better
We are higher
We can't change the social order, right?
So don't fight
Don't call us wrong
For we are very very strong.

———•—•—•———

One Day

The world crawled to the shore,
Against huge waves of hatred and destruction,
She fought the sharp spikes
Of bigotry,
Her loss of freedom
Her loss of voice...
In a world where
Chaos ruled beneath
The artifice of beauty
Free movement and soaring high…
No longer a choice.

She spent hours, days, years,
Weeping grief-laden torrents of tears,
No-one would listen to her fears.
Despair is a dull ache,
Through which rage and determination flourish...
The sea will be calm one day, she assured herself,
The river will not overflow and flood,
People will make their choices, see
Reason and not shed blood.
One year slipped into the next,
Before the world stopped to think,
Rather than weep.
This time, I will

See the eternal sunrise,
And hold its beauty to keep.
Her foamy fingers made
Lace patterns on the sea shore,
Each one unique,
Each one promising...
An unknown yet better destiny.
The river, in its abundance,
Showed joy
As it gurgled and frothed
Its way across
Centuries of rocks and stones
Carving a future of resilience and peace...
One day.

Remember Me

Puja Roy

Remember Me

December 7, 2023

When you see a rainbow
Spread across the sky,
Think of its colours of hope, inclusion, exuberance...
And remember me.

Billions of stars dance and shine happily
On a clear, moonlit sky,
Pick the brightest, the naughtiest, the one least perfect,
Hold it in your hands,
Make a wish, fling it back into the sky...
And remember me.

The sun throws its
Rays of light
Onto a thriving earth.
Think of its power and omnipresence,
Its dignity and immortality...
And remember me.

I am a touch and breath away,
In the fragrance of frangipanis,
The salt of the ocean,
The flow of the brook.
I am the tumult of waterfalls,

The symphony of bird songs,
I am the power
In the flame of a candle.

I am a thought away,
My passion to live
Will carry on.

I am nowhere and everywhere...
When you reach out
To me in your thoughts,
I will be there through
Myriad ways and possibilities,
And we will walk ahead...
Together.

When things go dark
Hold the torch high in the sky...
And stride on.

And remember me.
Remember me.

About the Author

Puja Roy was born in Malaysia in the mid-1960s into a close-knit family consisting of her doctor father, Pranaba Kumar Roy, her mother, Aparajita Ray, talented in writing and singing, and three sisters. When her parents moved to Papua New Guinea in 1980, Puja accompanied them. At the International school in Port Moresby, Puja's talent in writing was recognised and encouraged by the teachers in high school, and she gradually blossomed into a confident young woman.

Following this, Puja applied and was admitted to the prestigious Loreto College, Kolkata, India, for an undergraduate degree majoring in English. Recognising a growing passion for addressing societal inequalities, she eventually went on to study at the Tata Institute of Social Sciences, Mumbai, and graduated with a master's degree in Social Work in 1990.

Thereafter followed years of working with many well-known global organisations in the areas of development and empowerment of women. In 1998, Puja authored a research-based article titled "Sanctioned Violence: Development and the Persecution of Women as Witches in South Bihar". This writing was published as part of a book and has been widely cited by researchers. Her work in South Asia also included fighting against the trafficking of women, and most recently, several years spent working towards eradicating child marriage and improving access to education for girls in Jharkhand.

Happily married to a supportive husband, Puja successfully juggled the demands of her career and raising a family of two children; a son and a daughter. Puja loved reading books and would find comfort in her vast collection of them, neatly displayed at home. Her profound love for animals made her a vegetarian by choice. Puja's greatest passion was travelling with her family, and she enjoyed planning journeys to destinations all over the world. Her love of collecting masks and turtle-related memorabilia from the places she visited was well known.

Puja always stood up for the rights of the more marginalised sections of society and did her best to help others in both personal and professional capacities. In times of joy, frustration, and outrage, Puja had the habit of penning her thoughts as poems in a notebook she always kept handy. She often shared these poems with her friends on social media, sometimes sparking off intellectual discussions. She had always expressed a strong wish to publish some of her poetry in a book. However, Puja passed away in July 2024, before she could fulfil this wish.

In the Fragrance of Frangipanis is a loving compilation of some of her work, so that her thoughts, observations, and convictions can be preserved as a legacy to her and be shared and appreciated by all. Puja is remembered by her husband, Prasenjit; her children, Anubhav and Anokhi; her sisters, Sumana, Sunrita, and Rumee; and a profoundly large number of others whose lives she touched in a meaningful way.

93